CONSTELLATIONS

Consultant: Geoff Chester
Illustrators: Carol Schwartz, Robert Cremins, Stuart Armstrong

Published by
The National Geographic Society
John M. Fahey, Jr., President and Chief Executive Officer
Gilbert M. Grosvenor, Chairman of the Board
Nina D. Hoffman, Senior Vice President
William R. Gray, Vice President and Director, Book Division

Staff for this Book
Barbara Brownell, Director of Continuities
Marianne R. Koszorus, Senior Art Director
Toni Eugene, Editor
Alexandra Littlehales, Art Director
Patricia Daniels, Writer-Researcher
Susan V. Kelly, Illustrations Editor
Sharon Kocsis Berry, Illustrations Assistant
Mark A. Caraluzzi, Director of Direct Response Marketing
Heidi Vincent, Product Manager
Vincent P. Ryan, Manufacturing Manager
Lewis R. Bassford, Production Project Manager

Visit our Web site at www.nationalgeographic.com

Library of Congress Catalog Card Number: 132922
ISBN: 0-7922-3457-X

Color separations by Quad Graphics, Martinsburg, West Virginia
Printed in Mexico by R.R. Donnelley & Sons Company

CONSTELLATIONS

Patricia Daniels

NATIONAL
GEOGRAPHIC
SOCIETY

INTRODUCTION

Can you name the stars that shine over your house every night? Few people can. But this was not always so. Ancient Babylonians, Greeks, Native Americans, and other peoples knew the skies well. Seeing pictures in the stars, they gave them names from their own myths. These star pictures are called constellations.

Today there are 88 constellations. You can see 54 of them from the Northern Hemisphere (the northern half) of the Earth. Twelve constellations are signs of the zodiac, the famous set of animals and scale for weighing things that make up a year. You can also see star shapes, such as the Big Dipper, inside constellations. These shapes are called asterisms.

In modern astronomy, each constellation includes not only the stars of its shape, but also other stars, huge star groups called galaxies, and yet more objects around the shape. Astronomers have mapped the sky so that every visible object belongs to a constellation.

On clear dark nights, you may see a fuzzy band of light crossing the sky. That band is called the Milky Way. It is the main part of our galaxy, where stars are thickest. All the stars you see with the naked eye belong to our own galaxy, which was named after the Milky Way.

Because our planet rotates, the constellations rise and set just as the sun and moon do. And because our planet moves through space as it circles the sun, we see different constellations as a year passes. Each constellation has a season when it is highest in the sky. Before you go out, check the star charts (pages 8-15). They will show you where constellations are at different times of the year.

SKY-WATCHING

All you really need to enjoy stars are your eyes and a clear night. Still, it helps to be prepared. Here are some tips:

• **Avoid lights.** Do your sky-watching as far from city, street, or house lights as possible. Then give your eyes 15 or 20 minutes to adapt to darkness.

• **Use a red flashlight.** If you use a flashlight to look at this book, tape red plastic across the front of the bulb to keep its light as dim as possible.

• **Watch out for planets.** Some of the sky's brightest lights are planets, not stars. Check the weather page of your newspaper for planet locations.

• **Give it time.** You'll see right away that constellations rarely look like the animals or people they're named for. Become familiar with the sky over many nights.

• **Begin with easy shapes.** Orion and Ursa Major (the Big Dipper) are two bright, easy-to-recognize constellations. Once you can find those, you can move on to others.

HOW TO USE THIS BOOK

This book covers 29 easily seen northern constellations, in alphabetical order, followed by one famous southern constellation. A guide to pronouncing each constellation appears below its name. "Find It" helps you locate the constellation and shows how big it is next to your outstretched hands. The "Field Notes" entry gives you an extra fact about it. Photos of the constellations have lines laid over them to show their shapes. "What You Will See" tells what's visible with your eyes or instruments. A few objects, such as galaxies, clusters of stars, or the huge clouds of gas and dust called nebulae, (NE-byuh-lie) have names like M31. These come from a list called the Messier Catalog. If a word is unfamiliar, look it up in the Glossary on page 76.

STAR CHARTS

charts for February 15, 9 p.m.

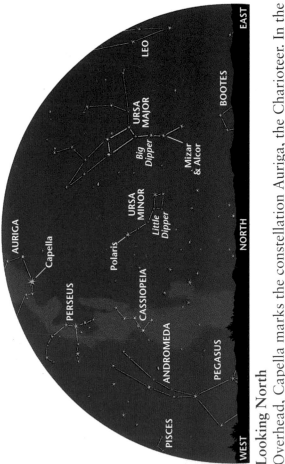

Looking North

Overhead, Capella marks the constellation Auriga, the Charioteer. In the west, Perseus, the Hero, stands above Cassiopeia, the Queen. The Little Dipper swings from Polaris, while the Big Dipper rises in the northeast.

FOR WINTER

Looking South

Orion, the Hunter, stands out in the winter sky. Around him are Taurus, the Bull; Gemini, the Twins; and Canis Major, the Great Dog. Look for Sirius in Canis Major—Sirius is the brightest star in the sky.

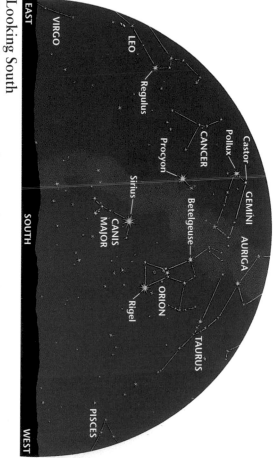

EAST

VIRGO

LEO

Regulus

CANCER

Pollux

Castor

GEMINI

Procyon

Sirius

Betelgeuse

AURIGA

CANIS MAJOR

SOUTH

ORION

Rigel

TAURUS

PISCES

WEST

STAR CHARTS

charts for May 15, 9 p.m.

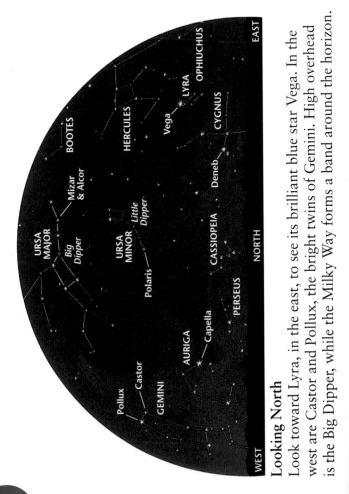

Looking North

Look toward Lyra, in the east, to see its brilliant blue star Vega. In the west are Castor and Pollux, the bright twins of Gemini. High overhead is the Big Dipper, while the Milky Way forms a band around the horizon.

FOR SPRING

Looking South

Leo crouches overhead, marked by its "backward-question-mark" shape. Two bright stars stand out in the sky—white Spica, in Virgo, and the orange star Arcturus, in Bootes.

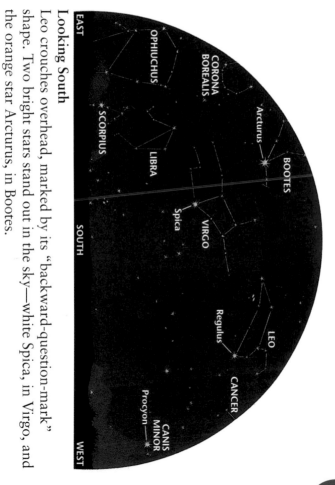

STAR CHARTS

charts for August 15, 9 p.m.

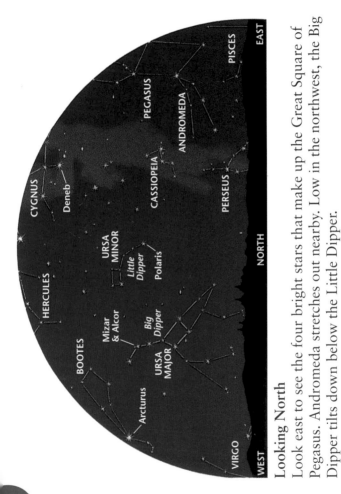

Looking North

Look east to see the four bright stars that make up the Great Square of Pegasus. Andromeda stretches out nearby. Low in the northwest, the Big Dipper tilts down below the Little Dipper.

FOR SUMMER

Looking South

Three piercingly bright stars—Altair, Vega, and Deneb (on the Looking North chart) form the Summer Triangle. Scorpius, Capricornus, and Sagittarius are low in the sky.

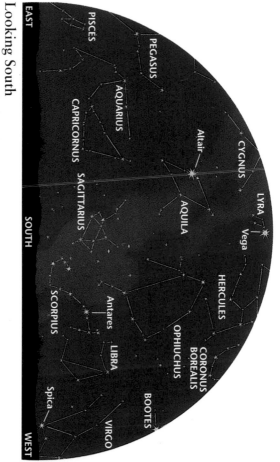

EAST

SOUTH

WEST

PISCES

PEGASUS

AQUARIUS

CAPRICORNUS

SAGITTARIUS

Altair

CYGNUS

LYRA

Vega

AQUILA

SCORPIUS

Antares

LIBRA

Spica

VIRGO

BOOTES

OPHIUCHUS

CORONUS
BOREALIS

HERCULES

STAR CHARTS

charts for November 15, 9 p.m.

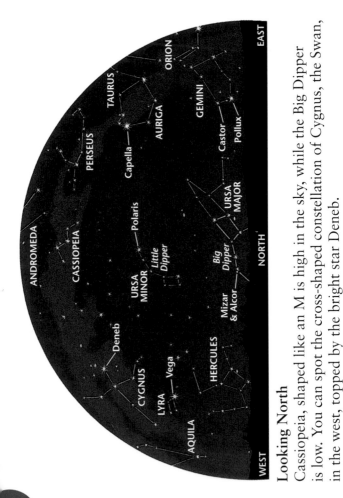

Looking North

Cassiopeia, shaped like an M is high in the sky, while the Big Dipper is low. You can spot the cross-shaped constellation of Cygnus, the Swan, in the west, topped by the bright star Deneb.

FOR FALL

Looking South

Look to the east for the bright stars of Orion rising above the horizon. The Great Square of Pegasus is now nearly overhead. Far to the west, the brilliant star Altair marks Aquila, the Eagle.

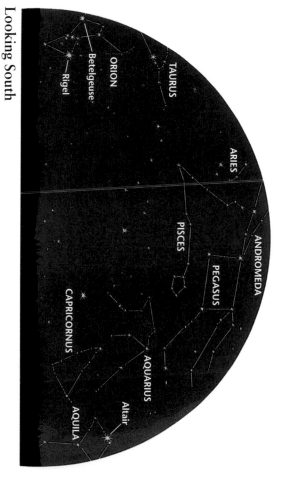

TAURUS

ORION
Betelgeuse
Rigel

ARIES

ANDROMEDA

PISCES

PEGASUS

CAPRICORNUS

AQUARIUS

AQUILA

Altair

ANDROMEDA

This V-shaped constellation was named after a princess in Greek myth. When you find Andromeda, look for the nearby Andromeda Galaxy, home to 200 billion stars.

FIND IT:
Looking north in the fall, find the curving V of Andromeda opening up toward the east.

WHAT YOU WILL SEE:

✳ WITH YOUR EYES
The Andromeda Galaxy, a fuzzy patch near Andromeda's knee, is the most distant object visible to the naked eye.

✳ THROUGH BINOCULARS
See an open cluster—a loose collection of stars—near Andromeda's lower left leg.

✳ THROUGH A TELESCOPE
A double star forms Andromeda's lower foot. A double star is a pair of stars that seem so close that they look like one.

The bright star Alpheratz, upper right, marks Andromeda's head. Her body and legs trail off to the left.

AQUARIUS

This sprawling constellation has always been connected with water in one way or another. Egyptians believed the figure was emptying his jar into the Nile River.

FIND IT:
Facing south in fall, look toward the horizon to find Aquarius. It is marked by a circle of stars at either end.

WHAT YOU WILL SEE:

✷ WITH YOUR EYES
In the middle of Aquarius lies a Y-shaped asterism known as the Water Jar.

✷ THROUGH BINOCULARS
Look for the Helix Nebula just below the constellation. This big nebula is a ring of gas from a dying star.

✷ THROUGH A TELESCOPE
Find a globular cluster—a tight, ball-like group of stars—above the western circle of Aquarius.

FIELD NOTES

A meteor shower,
shooting stars
that are really tiny
bits of a comet,
begins in Aquarius
every July 27.

The Y-shaped
Water Jar marks
the central part
of Aquarius.
Not all the
constellation is
visible in this
photograph.

AQUILA

Many old civilizations imagined this constellation as an eagle. To the Greeks, Aquila was the noble bird that carried the god Zeus's thunderbolts.

Altair, top center, mark's Aquila's head, while the stars of this constellation's outstretched wings form a diamond shape.

WHAT YOU WILL SEE:

✳ WITH YOUR EYES

Eta Aquilae, on Aquila's wing, is a variable star. A variable star is one that brightens and dims over time.

✳ THROUGH BINOCULARS

An open cluster of about 40 stars floats under Aquila's right wing.

✳ THROUGH A TELESCOPE

Find a double star near the eagle's tail and another under its left wing.

FIELD NOTES

Apollo astronauts used Altair, one of the brightest stars, to help them find their way to the moon.

21

ARIES

This little constellation is important as one of the 12 signs of the zodiac. The sign of Aries, the Ram, covers the part of the year from March 21 to April 20.

FIND IT:
Look toward the south in late fall or early winter. A bent line of stars marks the small form of Aries.

WHAT YOU WILL SEE:

✳ **WITH YOUR EYES**
Aries' brightest star, Hamal, is a huge red star that looks yellow to the eye.

✳ **THROUGH BINOCULARS**
Lambda Arietis, near Hamal, is a double star.

✳ **THROUGH A TELESCOPE**
The two bright white stars of Gamma Arietis were identified in 1664. It was one of the first double stars ever seen through a telescope.

Shaped like a broken stick, Aries can be seen in the center of the photo above.

AURIGA

One of the oldest
constellations, Auriga was
named 4,000 years ago.
It is supposed to show a
chariot driver or a herder
holding a goat.

FIND IT:
As you face south in the
winter, Auriga's bright star
Capella is almost overhead
against the Milky Way.

WHAT YOU WILL SEE:

✳ WITH YOUR EYES
Capella, a gigantic yellow star, is
known as the "she-goat star."

✳ THROUGH BINOCULARS
The open star cluster M37, just west of
the constellation, has 150 members
grouped around a red central star.

✳ THROUGH A TELESCOPE
Look for bright stars in the shape of a
cross in a small cluster in the center of
the constellation.

Every 27 years, the double star Epsilon Aurigae darkens when its dusty companion passes in front of it.

Marked by the huge star Capella, at upper left in the photo, Auriga rises above the horizon.

BOOTES

This summer constellation is said to show the farmer who invented the plow. In some stories he hunts the bears of the constellations Ursa Major and Ursa Minor.

FIND IT:
Facing south in summer, look almost straight up to find brilliant Arcturus at the constellation's bottom.

WHAT YOU WILL SEE:

✴ **WITH YOUR EYES**
Arcturus is a cool, yellow-orange giant star only 37 light-years from our sun. A light-year is the distance light travels in a year—about six trillion miles.

✴ **THROUGH BINOCULARS**
Mu Bootis is a triple star—three stars orbiting each other.

✴ **THROUGH A TELESCOPE**
Look for the double star Kappa Bootis in the upper right of the constellation.

Anchored by Arcturus, at right, Bootes opens out toward the left in an ice-cream-cone shape.

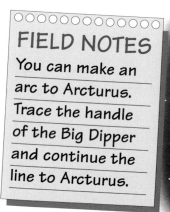

You can make an arc to Arcturus. Trace the handle of the Big Dipper and continue the line to Arcturus.

CANCER

This little constellation honors a brave crab who fought the legendary strongman Hercules—and got stomped. Two of its end stars mark the crab's claws.

FIND IT:
Face south and look overhead in spring. Dim Cancer opens out toward the west.

WHAT YOU WILL SEE:

✳ **WITH YOUR EYES**
Look for the open Beehive Cluster right in the middle of the crab's body.

✳ **THROUGH BINOCULARS**
Another open cluster, M67, can be seen near the crab's claw. Its stars are about ten billion years old.

✳ **THROUGH A TELESCOPE**
Zeta Cancri is a quadruple star— four stars circling each other in a complicated dance.

Just above the planet Jupiter, the brightest point in this photo, are two central stars of Cancer and the Beehive Cluster.

CANIS MAJOR

Most stories say that this bright, easily seen winter constellation shows the favorite dog of Orion, a nearby constellation also known as the Hunter.

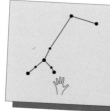

FIND IT:
Facing south in winter, look for Canis Major's brilliant star Sirius near the Milky Way.

WHAT YOU WILL SEE:

✳ WITH YOUR EYES
Sirius, only 8.7 light-years from Earth, is the brightest star in our skies. It has a dimmer companion called the Pup.

✳ THROUGH BINOCULARS
Look for a large open cluster with a red central star just south of Sirius.

✳ THROUGH A TELESCOPE
A cluster surrounds the star Tau Canis Majoris in the southwest corner of the constellation.

With Sirius
on its shoulder,
upper right,
Canis Major
seems to run
across the sky.

CANIS MINOR

KAY-*NIS* MY-*NER*

Canis Minor is Orion's smaller hunting dog. It romps behind him, keeping to one side of the Milky Way while the Great Dog runs on the other side.

FIND IT:
Face south in late winter to find the Little Dog east of the Milky Way. Look for its bright star Procyon.

WHAT YOU WILL SEE:

✳ WITH YOUR EYES
Procyon is a brilliant yellow star. It is only 11 light-years away from Earth.

✳ THROUGH BINOCULARS
Canis Minor's second brightest object is a star known as Gomeisa. You can find it just northwest of Procyon.

✳ THROUGH A TELESCOPE
Just up from Gomeisa, look for Dolidze 26, a small, stretched-out cluster of stars.

Canis Minor has only two bright stars: Procyon, at the center of the photo, and Gomeisa, below it.

○○○○○○○○○○○○○○
FIELD NOTES
Three bright stars,
Procyon, Sirius,
and Betelgeuse
(BEE-tul-joos)—
form the Winter
Triangle asterism.

CAPRICORNUS

KAP-REH-COR-NUS

Capricornus is spread out like a crooked grin in the sky. This dim constellation has been viewed as a goat or goat-fish in the zodiac since ancient times.

FIND IT:
In early fall, look south about halfway up from the horizon to find the bent triangle of Capricornus.

WHAT YOU WILL SEE:

✹ WITH YOUR EYES
The brightest star, Algedi, is an optical double—two stars that look close but are really different distances from Earth.

✹ THROUGH BINOCULARS
The constellation's second brightest star, is a true double star—that is, a pair of stars that circle each other.

✹ THROUGH A TELESCOPE
A globular cluster, M30, floats just south of the goat's tail.

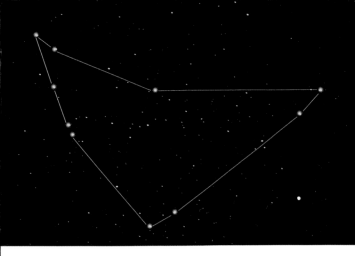

FIELD NOTES

Capricornus may show the goat-god Pan, who changed partly into a fish to escape the monster Typhon.

Capricornus's stars aren't bright, but they are easy to find because they are in an uncrowded area of the sky. The bright spot at right is Saturn.

CASSIOPEIA

Cassiopeia was Andromeda's mother. Romans believed that Cassiopeia was hung upside down in the skies as punishment for boasting about her own beauty.

FIND IT:
Looking north in late fall, find the M shape of Cassiopeia outlined against the Milky Way.

WHAT YOU WILL SEE:

✴ WITH YOUR EYES
At the center of the M is an irregular variable, a star that brightens and dims at different times over the years.

✴ THROUGH BINOCULARS
Find the open cluster M52 by tracing a line below the first leg of the M.

✴ THROUGH A TELESCOPE
Above the center of the M is a star cluster called the Night Owl because it looks like the eyes and wings of a bird.

Cassiopeia forms a striking zigzag against a starry background.

CORONA BOREALIS

 Many civilizations have described this clear half circle of stars as a crown. To some Native Americans, though, the shape was a circle of girls dancing.

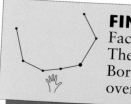

FIND IT:
Face south in early summer. The circlet of Corona Borealis is almost directly overhead.

WHAT YOU WILL SEE:

✳ WITH YOUR EYES
The brightest star of Corona Borealis, known as the Gem, is a double star.

✳ THROUGH BINOCULARS
Rho Coronae Borealis, above the constellation's center, is a variable star.

✳ THROUGH A TELESCOPE
The stars in a double star under the constellation are so close that one pulls gas from the other, building up mass until it explodes—then grows again.

The seven main stars of Corona Borealis form a small C that is easily seen on summer nights.

FIELD NOTES

Astronomers think sooty clouds of carbon erupt from Rho Coronae Borealis at times, blocking its light.

CYGNUS

With its spread wings and long neck, Cygnus, the Swan, is the rare constellation that actually looks like its name. Cygnus is one of the clearest shapes in the summer sky.

Cygnus soars down the river of the Milky Way with its brightest star, Deneb, at the top. Its wing tips are outside the photograph.

FIND IT:
In summer, face south and look overhead to find the cross-like shape of Cygnus against the Milky Way.

WHAT YOU WILL SEE:

✳ WITH YOUR EYES
Deneb, on the swan's tail, is 60,000 times as bright as our sun.

✳ THROUGH BINOCULARS
The center of the constellation, where it crosses the Milky Way, is especially rich in stars.

✳ THROUGH A TELESCOPE
The Veil Nebula, under the swan's eastern wing, may be the beautiful remains of a supernova.

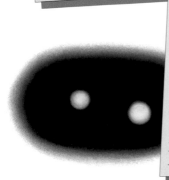

FIELD NOTES
Albireo, at the swan's head, is a gorgeous double star. One of the pair is blue, and the other is gold.

41

GEMINI

Gemini's twin stars are named after Greek heroes Castor and Pollux, who sailed on the legendary ship *Argo*. This sign of the zodiac means good luck to sailors.

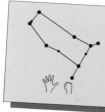

FIND IT:
Look overhead, facing south, in winter. Gemini's bright pair of stars is fairly easy to see.

WHAT YOU WILL SEE:

✳ WITH YOUR EYES
Compare Castor and Pollux, Gemini's brightest stars, to see that Pollux is slightly brighter.

✳ THROUGH BINOCULARS
An open star cluster, M35, lies near the twins' feet.

✳ THROUGH A TELESCOPE
With a strong telescope you can see details of the "face" of the blue-green Clownface Nebula just under Gemini.

Stars Castor, at top left of this photo, and Pollux, underneath it, mark the twins' heads at left; their bodies stretch to the right.

FIELD NOTES

Greek myths say that Castor and Pollux, twin sons of the god Zeus, were born from a swan's eggs.

HERCULES

This summer constellation is named for the mighty hero of Greek and Roman legend. It is big and dim, as befits its muscular, but none-too-bright subject.

FIND IT:
Facing south in summer, find Hercules overhead, his arms stretching toward the south.

WHAT YOU WILL SEE:

✳ WITH YOUR EYES
Ras Algethi, brightest point in Hercules, is a double star. One member is orange red and the other blue green.

✳ THROUGH BINOCULARS
Look for the the big, brilliant Hercules cluster, M13, on the eastern edge of the central square of Hercules.

✳ THROUGH A TELESCOPE
The cluster M92, under Hercules' body, is small but has a bright core.

44

The most famous globular, or ball-like, cluster of stars in the northern sky is the Hercules Cluster.

The four stars that mark the corners of the strongman's body, at left, form an asterism known as the Keystone.

LEO

The shape of Leo reminded many ancient people of a lion with an upright head. The brightest star in the constellation, Regulus, was called "the heart of the lion."

FIND IT:

In spring, look south of the Big Dipper. The stars of Leo's head form a backward question mark.

WHAT YOU WILL SEE:

✳ **WITH YOUR EYES**
Leo's chest is marked by the blue-white double star Regulus.

✳ **THROUGH BINOCULARS**
The red variable star R Leonis, in front of Regulus, brightens and dims over a $10\frac{1}{2}$-month period.

✳ **THROUGH A TELESCOPE**
Three galaxies huddle together under the lion's belly. Two of them are spiral shaped, like our Milky Way galaxy.

Bright Regulus, at lower right in the photo, is at the bottom of Leo's well-known sickle-shaped asterism.

FIELD NOTES
Some people have suggested that Leo inspired the form of the famous Sphinx statue in Egypt.

LIBRA

Libra, the Balance, is the only constellation of the 12 in the zodiac that is not an animal. Named in Roman times, it shows the balancing scales of the goddess of justice.

FIND IT:
Face south and look toward the horizon in summer. The peak of Libra's scales points west.

WHAT YOU WILL SEE:

✳ WITH YOUR EYES
Libra's brightest star, which has the wonderful Arab name Zubenelgenubi, is a wide double star.

✳ THROUGH BINOCULARS
Delta Librae, just above the scales, is a variable star that changes in brightness every 2.3 days.

✳ THROUGH A TELESCOPE
A globular cluster under the scales looks like a dim glow through small 'scopes.

Libra's scales look like a flattened triangle with two chains dangling from its tips. The lower chain is not visible in this photo.

LYRA

Lyra, the Lyre, is small but bright. It represents the little harp carried by the Greek musician Orpheus. The god Zeus placed the lyre in the sky to honor the musician.

FIND IT:
In summer, face south and look overhead. Find Lyra's brightest star, Vega, at the constellation's northern end.

WHAT YOU WILL SEE:

✳ WITH YOUR EYES
Vega is the second brightest star in the northern sky.

✳ THROUGH BINOCULARS
Beta Lyrae is a double star that brightens and dims every 13 days.

✳ THROUGH A TELESCOPE
Near Vega is Epsilon Lyrae, a double-double star. Through binoculars a double-double looks like two stars; a telescope reveals two pairs of stars.

Find Vega, at the
top of the photo,
and then look
down and right to
see the squashed
rectangle of Lyra.

OPHIUCHUS

Ophiuchus, or the Serpent Bearer, represents a Greek healer named Asclepius. The figure is usually shown holding Serpens, a serpent constellation that lies nearby.

FIND IT:
Look south toward the horizon in summer to see the large, dim shape of Ophiuchus.

WHAT YOU WILL SEE:

✳ WITH YOUR EYES
The blue star Alpha Ophiuchi marks the Serpent Bearer's head.

✳ THROUGH BINOCULARS
Look for an open cluster next to the Serpent Bearer's shoulder. You should be able to pick out separate stars in the cluster with powerful binoculars.

✳ THROUGH A TELESCOPE
Inside the body of Ophiuchus, find the loose globular cluster M10.

Ophiuchus looks less like a person than a tall house with a bright star at the peak.

FIELD NOTES

Fast-moving Barnard's Star, in Ophiuchus, changes position over time against background stars.

ORION

 Big, beautiful Orion may be the sky's most recognizable constellation. Greek myths tell us that this boastful hunter was killed by Scorpius, the scorpion.

FIND IT:
In winter, look south toward the horizon. The three stars of Orion's belt are easy to pick out.

WHAT YOU WILL SEE:

✳ WITH YOUR EYES
At Orion's right foot is a blazing blue-white supergiant star.

✳ THROUGH BINOCULARS
Look for the Great Nebula under Orion's belt. This glowing orange dust cloud is a birthplace of stars.

✳ THROUGH A TELESCOPE
Four bright young stars called the Trapezium lie at the core of the Great Nebula. Their energy lights it up.

Orion, at right in the photo above, has a wonderfully clear shape. Betelgeuse marks his shoulder and Rigel, his foot. A starry sword hangs below the Hunter's belt.

FIELD NOTES

Betelgeuse is a red supergiant. It is more than 600 million miles wide—bigger than the orbit of Mars.

PEGASUS

Pegasus, the Winged Horse, is named for a flying horse owned by the Greek hero Perseus. Pegasus soars upside down, legs outstretched, near the constellation of its master.

FIND IT:
In fall, look overhead facing south. Find four stars that form a distinct square in the sky.

WHAT YOU WILL SEE:

✳ WITH YOUR EYES
Beta Pegasi, also called Scheat, is a slightly variable star.

✳ THROUGH BINOCULARS
The globular cluster M15, near the horse's head, is a showy group of stars with a tight, bright core.

✳ THROUGH A TELESCOPE
Fifty million light-years away, a spiral-shaped galaxy under the horse's legs resembles the Andromeda galaxy.

Marked by a square of stars on the left, the constellation Pegasus shows only the front half of the legendary horse.

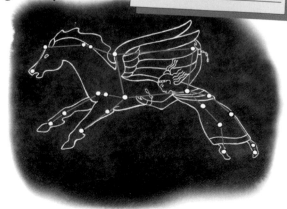

PERSEUS

The constellation Perseus can be found next to Andromeda, the maiden he rescued from a sea monster. Perseus is holding the head of the snake-haired monster Medusa.

FIND IT:
Face north in winter and look overhead. The constellation Perseus crosses the Milky Way.

WHAT YOU WILL SEE:

✴ WITH YOUR EYES
Algol, which marks Medusa's eye, is a variable star that grows suddenly dimmer about every three days.

✴ THROUGH BINOCULARS
Above Perseus' upraised sword lie two of the sky's brightest open clusters.

✴ THROUGH A TELESCOPE
Near Algol you should be able to pick out individual stars in the bright, open cluster M34.

Perseus, with its brightest star, Alpha Persei, at left center, sprawls across a rich field of stars.

○○○○○○○○○○○○○
FIELD NOTES
Variable star Algol was known as the Demon to Arab astronomers because it seemed to wink in the sky.

PISCES

To the Greeks, this large, faint constellation showed the goddess Aphrodite and her son Eros, who both changed into fish connected by a cord.

FIND IT:
Facing south in winter, find a wide V shape with its brightest star at the bottom of the V.

WHAT YOU WILL SEE:

✳ WITH YOUR EYES
Look for the Circlet: a ring of five stars that make up the body of Pisces' western fish.

✳ THROUGH BINOCULARS
Zeta Piscium, halfway to the western fish, is a double star.

✳ THROUGH A TELESCOPE
The galaxy M74 is a large spiral. Through a good-size telescope you will see a bright center in a dimmer glow.

A small circle of stars (top center) marks one of the two fish of Pisces. The bright spot at lower right is the planet Jupiter.

SAGITTARIUS

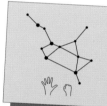 Sagittarius is big, bright, and full of interesting things to see. Its shape represents a centaur—a creature that is half man and half horse—shooting an arrow into space.

FIND IT:
Look south and low toward the horizon on a summer night. Sagittarius rests on top of the Milky Way.

WHAT YOU WILL SEE:

✳ WITH YOUR EYES
Look for the Teapot asterism, a kettle-shaped group of stars complete with spout and handle, in the western part of the constellation.

✳ THROUGH BINOCULARS
Lanes of dust split the Trifid Nebula, a cloud of gas and stars, into three parts.

✳ THROUGH A TELESCOPE
A bright star cluster, M22, is located north of the Teapot's handle.

62

The stars of the
Teapot, at center,
form the shape
of the centaur's
bow, all of the
constellation
visible here.

SCORPIUS

 This bright constellation with a curling tail is said to show the scorpion that killed Orion. For safety, the gods placed the scorpion across the sky from the hunter.

FIND IT:
Face south and look toward the horizon in summer. Orange Antares marks the scorpion's heart.

WHAT YOU WILL SEE:

✳ **WITH YOUR EYES**
The brightest star in Scorpius is the supergiant Antares. Its name means "rival of Mars," since its orange color matches that of the planet.

✳ **THROUGH BINOCULARS**
Find the globular cluster M4 just west of Antares.

✳ **THROUGH A TELESCOPE**
Two open clusters—M6 and M7—float northeast of the Scorpion's stinger.

The scorpion's body hangs down from Antares, the middle star of the three at top center. Its tail curves up like a hook.

⦿⦿⦿⦿⦿⦿⦿⦿⦿⦿⦿⦿⦿

FIELD NOTES

Constellations that cross the path of the Milky Way are often rich in nebulae and open clusters.

TAURUS

Orange Aldebaran and a group of stars called the Pleiades make Taurus easy to find. This sign of the zodiac is said to represent the god Zeus in the form of a bull.

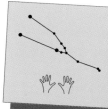

FIND IT:

In winter, face south and look overhead. Find the horn-like shape of Taurus opening toward the east.

WHAT YOU WILL SEE:

✳ WITH YOUR EYES
The giant orange star Aldebaran, 60 light-years away, is one eye of the bull.

✳ THROUGH BINOCULARS
The Pleiades, on the bull's shoulder, is the most famous star cluster. It contains more than 500 stars.

✳ THROUGH A TELESCOPE
Find the Crab Nebula, the glowing remains of a huge exploding star, near the tip of the bull's lower horn.

The stars in the center of this picture form the V of the bull's eyes and nose. The bright "star" toward the center is actually Mars.

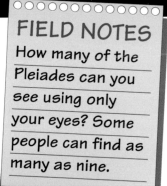

URSA MAJOR

One of the largest constellations in the sky, Ursa Major, or the Great Bear, contains the most famous of all asterisms, the Big Dipper.

FIND IT:
Face north in spring and look directly overhead. You'll see the Big Dipper hanging upside down.

WHAT YOU WILL SEE:

✳ WITH YOUR EYES
The star Mizar forms an optical double star in the middle of the dipper's handle.

✳ THROUGH BINOCULARS
Look for M81, a spiral galaxy above the Great Bear's head.

✳ THROUGH A TELESCOPE
Another galaxy, M101, is visible through low-power telescopes. This large, round spiral is 16 million light-years away.

The stars of
the Big Dipper,
brightest in
Ursa Major,
form the hind
part of the
bear's body.

○○○○○○○○○○○○

FIELD NOTES

According to
Iroquois legend,
seven starry
warriors hunt the
Great Bear all
summer long.

URSA MINOR

This easy-to-locate constellation is supposed to show the cub of the Great Bear, but it is better known to most sky-watchers as the Little Dipper.

FIND IT:
Look north in summer to find the Little Dipper shape of Ursa Minor. The bright star Polaris lies at one end.

WHAT YOU WILL SEE:

✳ **WITH YOUR EYES**
Follow the Little Dipper's handle to its end and you will see bright, white Polaris, the famous North Star.

✳ **THROUGH BINOCULARS**
Kochab, a reddish star almost as bright as Polaris, marks the top corner of the dipper's spoon.

✳ **THROUGH A TELESCOPE**
Gamma Ursae Minoris is a blue-and-orange double star.

With Polaris at lower left, Ursa Minor seems to stand on the tip of its tail.

FIELD NOTES

Polaris, the North Star, is almost directly over the North Pole. People can use it to find their way at night.

VIRGO

Virgo, the Maiden, is a sign of the zodiac and one of the oldest constellations. In many stories Virgo is a goddess of the harvest who holds a stalk of wheat.

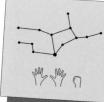

FIND IT:
In summer, face south and look toward the horizon. Look for Virgo's bright star Spica.

WHAT YOU WILL SEE:

✳ WITH YOUR EYES
Spica means "ear of wheat." It shines at the top of Virgo's wheat stalk and is one of the 20 brightest stars in the sky.

✳ THROUGH BINOCULARS
Northwest of the constellation's body you can see a beautiful group of galaxies known as the Virgo Cluster.

✳ THROUGH A TELESCOPE
Porrima, by Virgo's shoulder, is a yellow double star.

FIELD NOTES

A dark lane of dust surrounds Virgo's bright Sombrero Galaxy, making it look like a Mexican hat.

Anchored by Spica, below the orange dot of Mars, Virgo floats on her back, her head and feet outside the photograph.

73

CRUX

This brilliant cross of stars is the most famous of the Southern Hemisphere's constellations. Its upright portion points downward toward the South Pole.

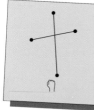

FIND IT:
You must be south of the Equator to see Crux. Its bright cross of stars lies within the Milky Way.

WHAT YOU WILL SEE:

✳ WITH YOUR EYES
Just east of the star Alpha Crux, better known as Acrux, is the well-named Coal Sack, a dark nebula.

✳ THROUGH BINOCULARS
The Jewel Box, on the eastern end of the cross, is a colorful star cluster that looks like a glittering treasure.

✳ THROUGH A TELESCOPE
Acrux is a brilliant double star that marks the bottom of the cross.

The four main
stars that make
up Crux form a
distinct cross or
diamond shape.

GLOSSARY

asterism A recognizable group of stars within a constellation.

cluster A group of stars that were formed about the same time. Clusters can be globular (ball-like) or open (loosely grouped).

constellation A pattern of stars named for an animal, person, or object; also, the area of sky around that pattern.

double star Two stars close together. True doubles are stars that orbit each other. Optical doubles look close together from Earth, but are not really linked.

galaxy An enormous group of stars held together by gravity.

giant star A huge, cool, swollen star at the end of its life span.

light-year The distance that light travels in one year (about six trillion miles).

meteor A bright streak of light, sometimes called a shooting star, made by bits of rock or ice speeding through the air.

nebula A cloud of gas or dust in space.

supergiant star An unusually big star at the end of its life span. A supergiant is larger than a giant.

supernova An exploding star.

variable star A star that changes in brightness.

white dwarf A small, hot, dim star at the end of its life span.

zodiac The group of twelve constellations that lies along the path followed by the sun, moon, and planets as the Earth moves around the sun.

INDEX OF
CONSTELLATIONS

ABOUT THE CONSULTANT

Geoff Chester is the Public Affairs Officer for the U. S. Naval Observatory in Washington, D.C. He serves as the spokesperson for the observatory, providing answers to the observatory's complex mission statement to the general public as well as to government and military leaders. Prior to joining the observatory in 1997, he worked for 19 years at the Smithsonian Institution's Albert Einstein Planetarium in positions that ranged from Special Effects Technician to Staff Astronomer. Geoff lives in Alexandria, Virginia, with his patient spouse, Laurie; children Abby and Nat; Bob the hermit crab; and seven telescopes.

PHOTOGRAPHIC CREDITS

front cover Bill & Sally Fletcher **back cover** Robert Cremins **half title** Bill & Sally Fletcher **title page** Alan Dyer **5** Bill & Sally Fletcher **17-73** all by J.B. Kaler **75** G. Dimijian **77** Alan Dyer **79** Bill & Sally Fletcher